The Riveting Red Rock of Sedona, Arizona

Joanne Kaminski

A non-fiction book for beginning readers

DEDICATION

I dedicate this book to my mom and my aunt. I had a wonderful vacation to Sedona, AZ back in 2011 and the memories will last me a lifetime.

Sedona was founded

In 1902

You don't want to miss it

Here's a great view

Sedona

Is in Arizona

That's two states left of

Oklahoma

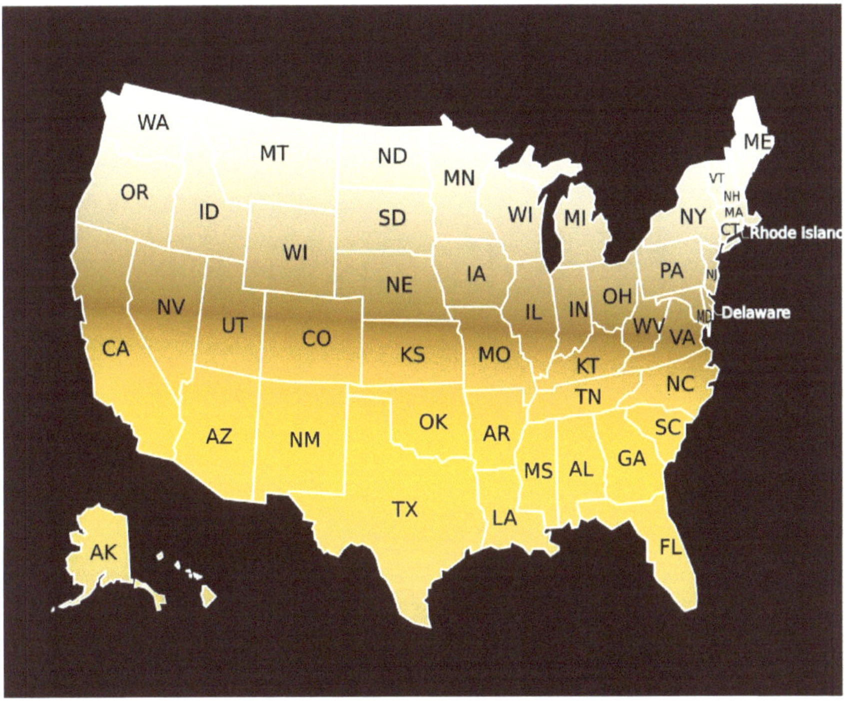
WA
MT
ND
MN
ME
VT
NH
MA
OR
ID
SD
WI
MI
NY
CT
Rhode Island
WI
IA
PA
NJ
NE
OH
NV
IL
IN
MD
Delaware
UT
WV
VA
CA
CO
KS
MO
KT
NC
TN
SC
OK
AR
AZ
NM
GA
MS
AL
TX
LA
AK
FL

The red on the rocks

Is really just rust

Don't worry

It won't combust

Bell Rock

Looks just like a bell

If you stare at it

You will be under a spell

Cathedral Rock

Looks like some churches

A great place to thank God

And worship

Chapel of

The Holy Cross

Stands between

The great red rocks

Hiking is fun

Anytime of year

It will fill you

With lots of cheer

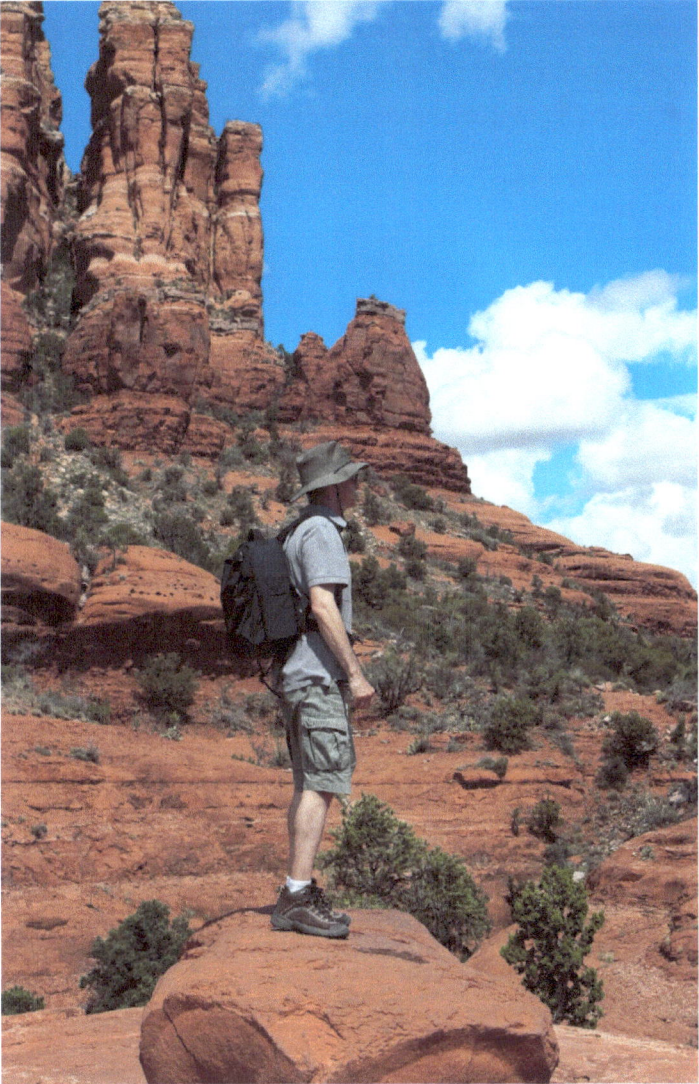

Meditating

Can be quite relaxing

It will calm your soul

From all the traveling

Faces in rocks

Can clearly be seen

Take a look

And you will know what I
mean

Flowers bloom

On Cacti in Spring

They look pretty

But they will sting

If you want to

Take your breath away

Look at a sunset

In the month of May

Nothing is sweeter

Than a hot air balloon

Through the red rocks

In June

Be careful

Not to fall into a cactus

When you land

It won't feel like a mattress

Tlaquepaque

Now try saying that

It's a mouthful

That you might have to work
at

TLAQUEPAQUE

There are many places

To go golfing

Look at the views

And take your next swing

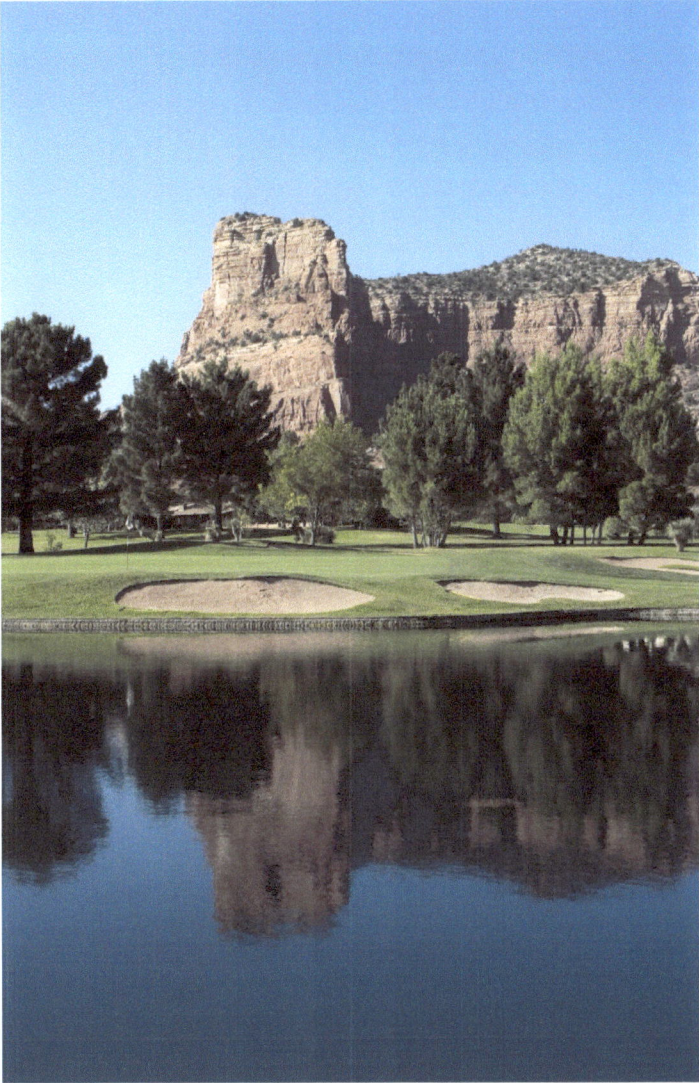

Midgely Bridge

Goes to Old Creek Canyon

Between Flagstaff and
Sedona

Take a companion

Even dogs

Find Sedona compelling

They could make this

Their next dwelling

Sometimes Sedona

Gets a sprinkling of snow

It may be well wanted

For all you know

Whenever you travel

It is usually warm

It's beautiful to look at

And be transformed

ABOUT THE AUTHOR

Joanne Kaminski is also known as the Skyping Reading Tutor. She started her own online reading tutoring company and helps kids close the reading gap quickly. During the day she gets to write books, visit schools, and take care of her family. At night she works with kids all over the world like Australia, Canada, and the United States from the west coast to the east coast.

Joanne began writing on her blog www.skypingreadingtutor.com in 2010. She fell in love with the writing process and now continues to write whenever she has the chance.

Joanne lives in Wisconsin with her husband and three girls. Her three girls were featured in her book Three Little Sisters Learn to Get Along. While they don't always get along, she loves spending time with them reading and traveling.

To learn more about Joanne Kaminski you can visit her website at www.joannekaminski.com. To learn more about online reading tutoring visit www.theskypingreadingtutor.com.

DID YOU ENJOY THIS BOOK
Please leave a review on amazon

Photo Credits

Each of the photos in this book were purchased from fotolia.com.

CHECK OUT THESE OTHER BOOKS BY JOANNE KAMINSKI

Three Little Sisters Learn to Get Along

31 Days to Become a Better Reader: Increasing your struggling reader's reading level

How to Raise Non-fiction Reading Levels

Job Security for Life in Teaching: How to become an online tutor

The Spectacular Natural Wonder: Niagara Falls

www.ingramcontent.com/pod-product-compliance
Lightning Source LLC
LaVergne TN
LVHW010023070426
835508LV00001B/31